Frogs

by
Gail Saunders-Smith

Pebble Books

an imprint of Capstone Press

Pebble Books are published by Capstone Press,
151 Good Counsel Drive, P.O. Box 669, Mankato, Minnesota 56002.
www.capstonepress.com

3 4 5 6 07 06 05

Library of Congress Cataloging-in-Publication Data
Saunders-Smith, Gail.
    Frogs / by Gail Saunders-Smith.
    p. cm.
    Summary: Describes and illustrates the life cycle of frogs.
    ISBN 1-56065-484-8 (hardcover)
    ISBN 1-56065-955-6 (paperback)
    1. Frogs—Life cycles—Juvenile literature. [1. Frogs.] I. Title.
QL668.E2S18 1997
597.8′9—dc21   97-8308
                                                                  CIP
                                                                   AC

Editorial Credits

Lois Wallentine, editor; Timothy Halldin and James Franklin, designers; Michelle L.
Norstad, photo researchers

Photo Credits

Dwight Kuhn, 14
Valan Photos/J.A. Wilkinson, cover; Jim Merli, 20; John Mitchell, 4, 6, 8, 10, 12;
    John Canclosi, 1, 18; Herman H. Giethoorn, 16

Table of Contents

4

Frogs lay eggs.

6

Eggs become tadpoles.

8

Tadpoles have tails.

Tadpoles grow back legs.

Tadpoles grow front legs.

The tails get shorter

15

16

and shorter

and shorter.

Tadpoles become frogs.

Words to Know

egg—the beginning stage of a frog

frog—a small green or brown animal that lives in the water and on land; a frog has webbed feet for swimming and long back legs for jumping

lay—to produce an egg or eggs

tadpole—the stage of a frog's growth between the egg and adult frog stages; tadpoles live in water

Read More

Lacey, Elizabeth. *The Complete Frog: A Guide for the Very Young Naturalist.* New York: Lothrop, Lee and Shepard Books, 1989.

Pascoe, Elaine. *Tadpoles.* Nature Close-Up. Woodbridge, Conn.: Blackbirch Press, 1997.

Pfeffer, Wendy. *From Tadpole to Frog.* Let's-Read-and-Find-Out Science. New York: HarperCollins, 1994.

Internet Sites

FactHound offers a safe, fun way to find Internet sites related to this book. All of the sites on FactHound have been researched by our staff.

Here's how:

1. Visit *www.facthound.com*

2. Type in this special code **1560654848** for age-appropriate sites. Or enter a search word related to this book for a more general search.

3. Click on the **Fetch It** button.

FactHound will fetch the best sites for you!

Note to Parents and Teachers

This book describes and illustrates the life cycle of a frog. The clear photographs support the beginning reader in making and maintaining the meaning of the text. The plural nouns and simple verbs match the photograph on each page. The limited repetition supports the beginning reader while offering new vocabulary. Children may need assistance in using the Table of Contents, Words to Know, Read More, Internet Sites, and Index/Word List sections of the book.

Index/Word List

Word Count: 28
Early-Intervention Level: 5